JEWISH HC
HEBREW CROSSWORD
PUZZLES FOR KIDS

This book belongs to: סֵפֶר זֶה כַּיָּךְ לְ:

_____

_____

Hebrew for US

Fun ideas for families and educators

Get in touch and stay up to date with
book releases and blog posts!

www.hebrewforus.com

@HebrewforUS

info@hebrewforus.com

The Hebrew Months

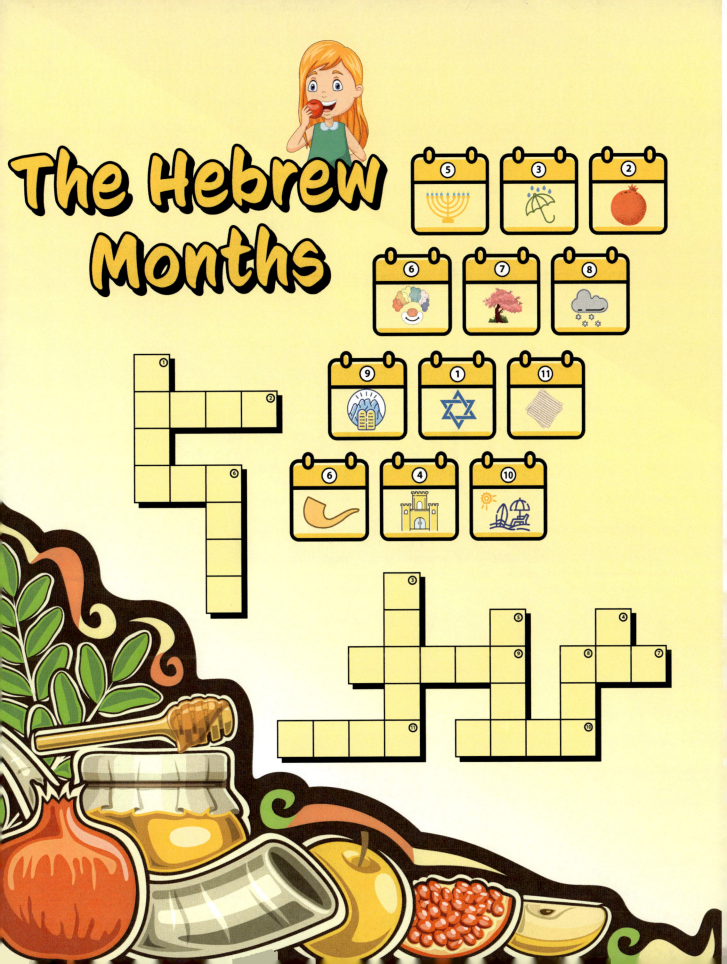

Tishrei Holidays

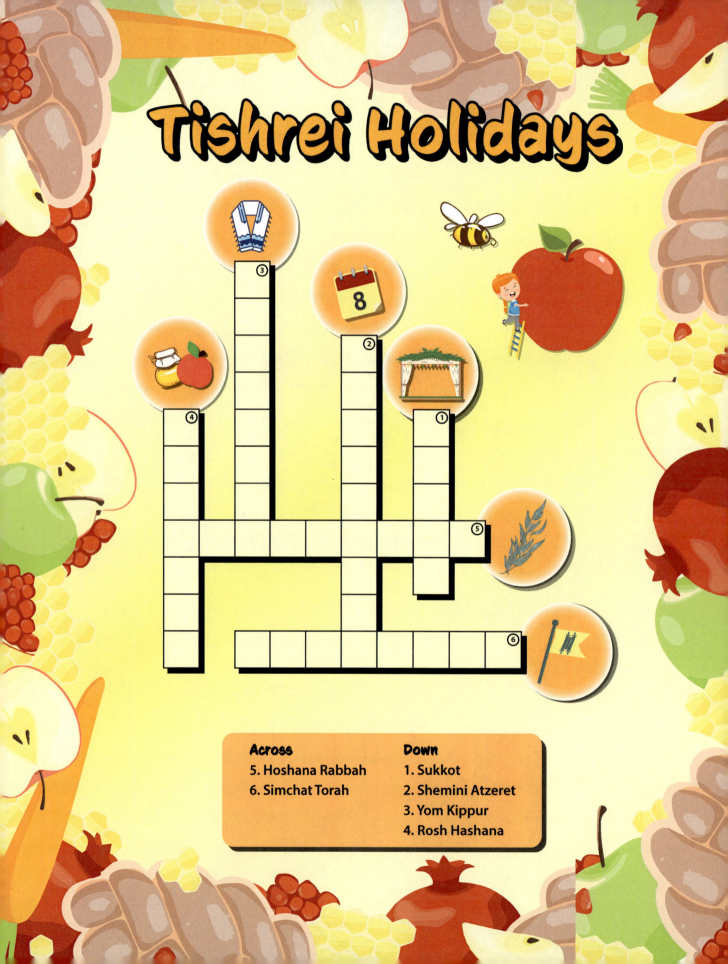

Across
5. Hoshana Rabbah
6. Simchat Torah

Down
1. Sukkot
2. Shemini Atzeret
3. Yom Kippur
4. Rosh Hashana

Rosh HaShanah

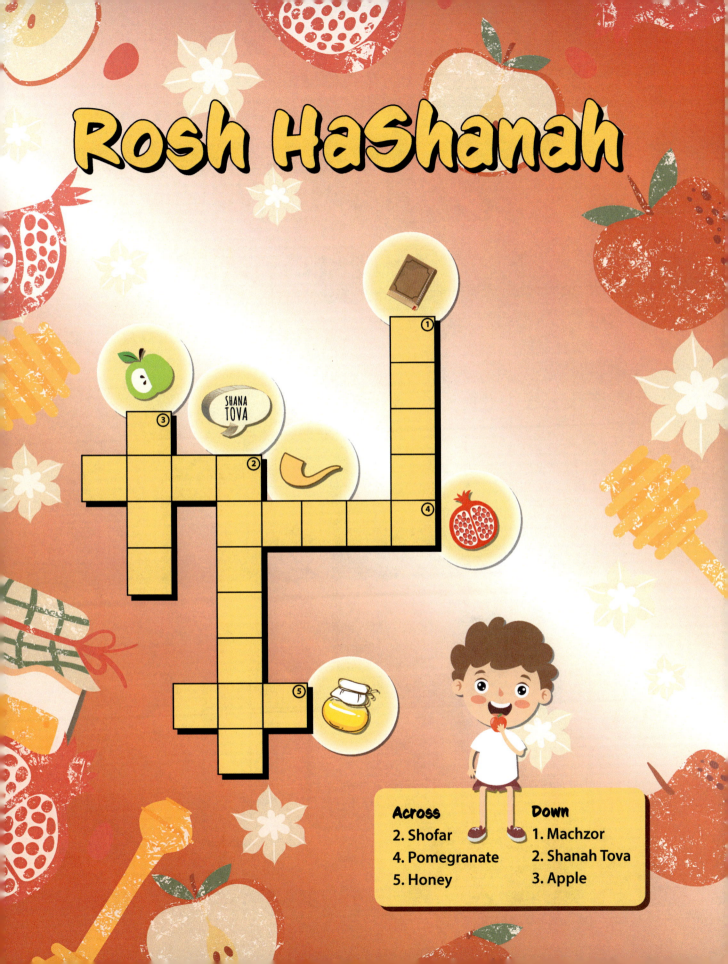

Across
2. Shofar
4. Pomegranate
5. Honey

Down
1. Machzor
2. Shanah Tova
3. Apple

Yom Kippur Prayers

חתימה
טובה אל

Across
3. Mincha
4. Arvit

Down
1. Ne'ila
2. Shacharit
3. Mussaf

Sukkot

Across
2. Etrog
4. Willow
7. Sukkah

Down
1. Decorations
2. Ushpizin
3. Lulav
5. Myrtle
6. Schach

Simchat Torah

Across
2. Genesis
5. Candy

Down
1. Torah
2. Songs
4. Going around

Hanukkah

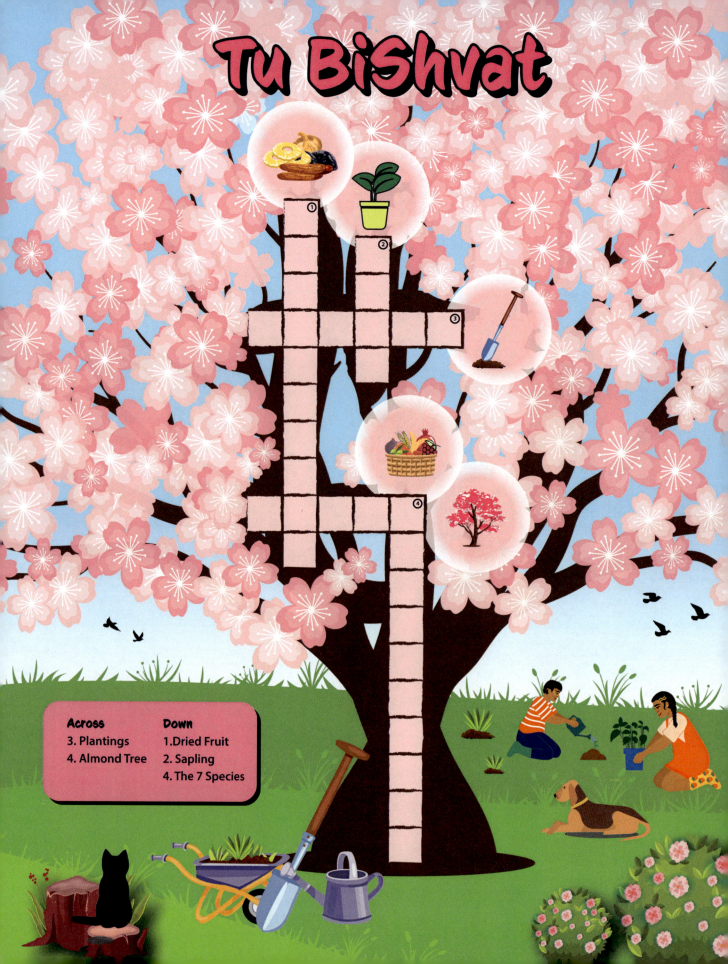

Tu BiShvat

Across
3. Plantings
4. Almond Tree

Down
1. Dried Fruit
2. Sapling
4. The 7 Species

The 7 Species

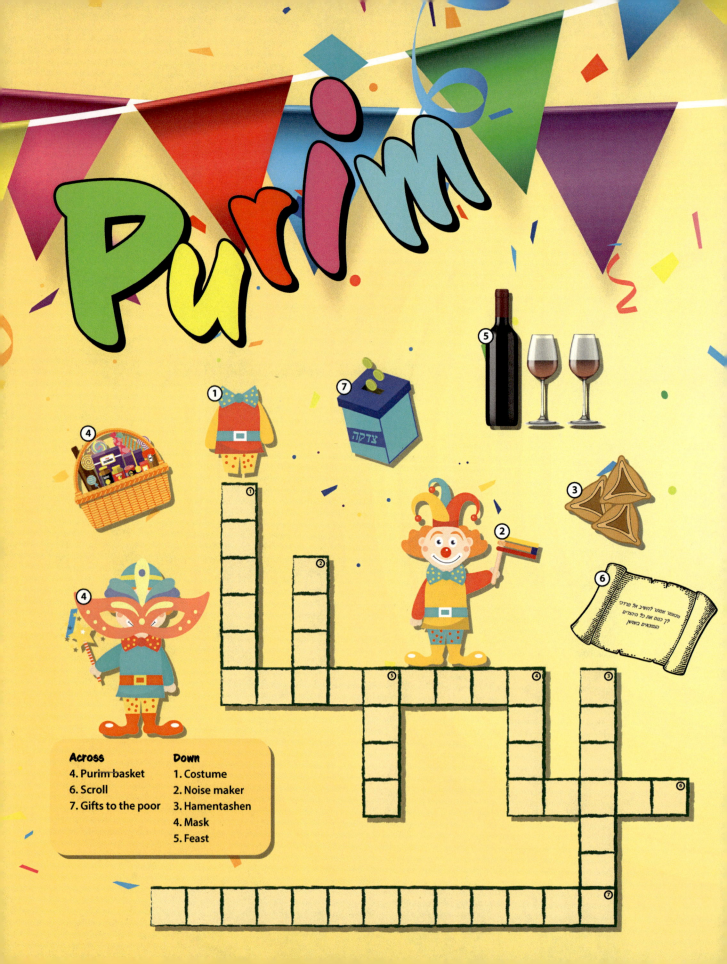

Purim

Across
4. Purim basket
6. Scroll
7. Gifts to the poor

Down
1. Costume
2. Noise maker
3. Hamentashen
4. Mask
5. Feast

Pesach

Across
2. Spring
5. Ma Nishtana
7. Afikoman
8. Plate

Down
1. Freedom
3. Moses
4. Egypt
5. Miriam
6. Haggadah

The Seder Plate

Yom HaAtzmaut

Across
3. Jerusalem
5. Hebrew
6. Jewish star

Down
1. Israeli flag
2. Tel-Aviv
4. HaTikva

Lag BaOmer

Shavuot

Across
4. Torah study
5. The 10 Commandments
6. Mount Sinai

Down
1. First-fruits
2. Cheesecake
3. Counting of the Omer

3 Regalim

Fast Days

Across
3. 10th of Tevet
5. Fast of Gedalia
6. 9th of Av

Down
1. Yom Kippur
2. 17th of Tamuz
4. Fast of Esther

Shabbat

Across
1. Synagogue
3. Candles
5. Challah

Down
2. Wine
4. Prayer book
6. Torah

Special Shabbatot

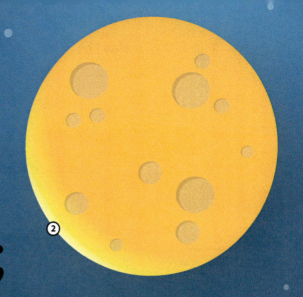

Across
1. Parah
3. Zakhor
4. Shekalim

Down
2. HaChodesh

The Hebrew Months

אתשרי
י
אדר
לול

חשון
שבט כסליו
תמוז
ניסן

Tishrei Holidays

יום
כיפור
שמיני
ראש השנה
סוכות
הושענא רבה
עצרת
שמחת תורה

Rosh HaShanah

מחזור
תפוח
שופר
רימונים
תקיעה
דבש

Yom Kippur Prayers

שחרית
נעילה
ערבית
מנחה
מוסף

Sukkot

קישוט
אתרוג
לולב
ושפיזין
ערבה
סוכה
הדס

Simchat Torah

תורה
בראשית
הקפות
ממתקים

Hanukkah

נרות
מכבים
סופגניה
מנורה
חנוכיה
לביבות
סביבון
שמן

דמי חנוכה

Tu BiShvat

פרי
שקד
נטיעות
עץ
שבעה
שקדיה
העצים

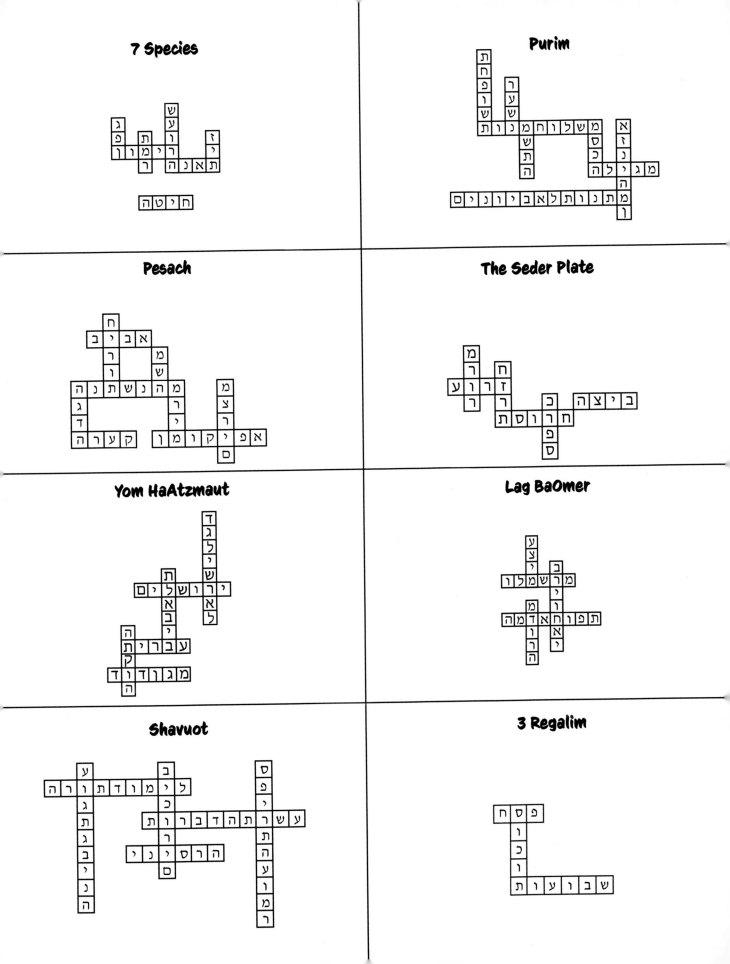

7 Species
Purim
Pesach
The Seder Plate
Yom HaAtzmaut
Lag BaOmer
Shavuot
3 Regalim

6 Fast Days

Shabbat

Special Shabbatot

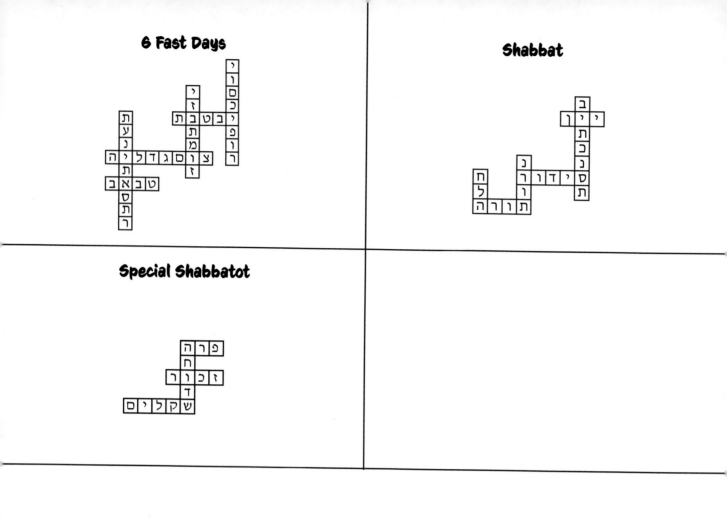